ELYSE HUDACSKO

Homeschool Activities for Teens

To my two favorite learners, Elisabeth and Natalie. xoxo

Contents

III   Kindness Activities

IV   Arts & Crafts Activities

V   Communications Activities

Preface

The two most dreaded words in the English language? "That's boring." Especially when escaping the lips of your resident homeschooled teenager regarding the educational opportunity you just presented them with.

In my homeschool, we never do anything that's boring! Because to me education is all about curiosity and freedom and creativity. Kids (well, actually, people) learn best when they are engaged.

Throughout my years of homeschooling middle and high school, I made it my mission to create learning opportunities for my daughters that helped them build skills in problem solving, determination, communication, kindness, and creativity while allowing them to feel full of excitement and joy. Some of the activities I came up with were total flops. The other 99 made it in to this book.

The activities in this book can be standalone or can be incorporated into other lessons you are doing. Some activities are quick and others take a while. Some require lots of materials and others little more than pencil and paper. Some activities provide detailed instructions and others point you in the direction to learn how to do them. Some of the activities will spark the interest of your teen and others are better left for another day. But I assure you that there are lots of activities in here that are perfect for your family!

I

Planning Activities

If there is one skill all teens should have before they leave the nest it is how to plan something, anything, from beginning to end.

The projects in this section will help your teen to conceptualize an idea, do research, identify necessary steps, schedule, manage, budget, and execute on time.

1

Produce a Short Film

One of my very favorite Unit Studies we ever did was film making. I loved giving my kids a simple prompt and watching them come back with an actual movie that made me either laugh or cry. Sometimes both.

While I had thought film making would engage their creative sides I had no idea how much it would engage their planning sides. They learned that they really had to plan out each scene and shot in great detail to convey the story they had envisioned.

In this project, teens will write, shoot, and edit a short film. This project can range from a 1 minute silent film to a more robust production complete with scripts, actors, and scene changes. Any format will prove to be entertaining!

GUIDELINES

- **Come up with a concept for a film.** *This can be the hardest step! If they are really stuck give them a random location, prop ,and line of dialogue and let them work for there.*
- **Storyboard the action.**
- **Create a production schedule.** *The schedule will need to include all the following steps as well as due dates.*

- **Write a script.** *Even if the movie is only a 1 minute silent film, you can actually script out the actions and emotions that are being portrayed. Search "how to write a script" to learn what the components of a script are!*
- **Gather props and costumes.**
- **Cast actors.** *Working with someone other than a little brother can add a level of professionalism to the project!*
- **Encourage your teen to learn proper camera techniques.** *While teens can certainly shoot a film using their own instincts, there are some tried and true methods to shooting a film to convey certain moods and emotions. There are plenty of YouTube videos available and short online film making courses. I have a fun Film Making Unit Study available at https://www.teacherspayteachers.com/Store/Elyse-Hudacsko.*
- **Shoot the film.**
- **Edit the film.** *There are loads of free editing apps available. We happen to love WeVideo.*
- **Add sound effects and music.**

2

Build an Animatronic

Every year for Halloween friends of ours create an amazing haunted experience in their yard. It is full of the scariest animatronics. And they have amazed my daughters since they were little.

One year we decided to try our hand at making our own. We ended up with a hissing cat that wagged it's tail and a bloody hand that rotated on the lawn. Maybe not the scariest of all Halloween decor but it was really cool to build our own.

In this project, teens will design and build an animatronic. (For Halloween or for any other reason they can come up with!) This project does require learning a bit about motors for even the mot basic animatronic and more curious teens can explore more advanced electronics.

GUIDELINES

- **Discuss the budget.**
- **Learn the basics of making a moving decoration.** *"Make" has a great overview of 4 simple and inexpensive animatronics. https://makezine.com/2017/10/25/4-animated-halloween-decorations-you-can-build-on-budget/. Teens can also get more sophisticated if they like!*

- **Design a decoration**. *They will need to design the internal structure as well as the outer decor.*
- **Create a materials list.**
- **Shop for materials in a store or online.**
- **Build the animatronic structure**. *Teens may need help with power tools!*
- **Add the decorative elements to the animatronic.**

3

Code a Video Game

One day my daughter looked at me and said, "I want to code a video game." I stared back blankly. I had no idea where to begin and was petrified to have to try to teach coding to my 13 year old.

But I did what all awesome homeschool moms do. I Googled it. And found a great program from MIT for first-time coders. My daughter taught herself the fundamentals of coding with the free program and built a few simple games that we all enjoyed playing. While my daughter decided she prefered playing video games to writing them, she certainly gained a basic understanding of how software comes to be.

In this project, teens will code a video game. The beauty of this project is that it can be a simple game (think Pong) or a complex game (like Minecraft) depending on your teen's skill level and interest.

GUIDELINES

- **Download programming software.** *For beginner programmers, I highly recommend Scratch from MIT. It is free and user friendly. Although you can certainly research other options and seasoned programmers can use what they already love.*

- **Learn how to program.** *If your teen does not know how to program, get them a book! If they choose to use Scratch to learn there are great books like "Scratch Programming for Teens" by Jerry Lee Ford, Jr. that will hep them learn the basics.*
- **Come up with a concept for a game they would like to build.** *Newer programmers will want to keep things simple for their first game!*
- **Design the elements of the game.**

1. **Main Character** – who are they? what do they look like? what powers do they have?
2. **Setting** – where is the game taking place?
3. **Goal** – what is the main character trying to achieve?
4. **Villains/Challenges** – who or what is trying to keep the main character from achieving their goal? what do they look like? what powers do they have?
5. **Levels** – what are the different scenarios the main character needs to get through?
6. **Scoring** – how is the game scored? are their bonuses? are their points or just a win?

- **Storyboard the game.** *By creating a picture and description for each level of the game, what has to be programmed becomes more clear. Encourage your teen to list out all the things that are going to have to happen. The more details, the better!*
- **Program and test.** *Remind your teen to test each level of their game before moving on. It is easier to fix mistakes right away then after you have coded a ton. They can treat each level of the game as it's own separate game!*

4

Create a Fairy Trail

When my daughters were little, they were obsessed with fairies. Which meant I was obsessed with fairies and always on the lookout for a fairy book or doll or outfit. One day I stumbled upon the mother load. A fairy trail.

I drove my two little fairies to the wooded trail and in we hiked. Moments later one of the girls spied a tiny house made of twigs and moss and stones. The prefect house for a fairy. Every few yards there was another delightful abode. Each one was made of natural materials. Some were little lean-tos with a little stick stool for a fairy to sit upon and others were elaborate homes with dining rooms, living rooms, hammocks, and feather beds!

Years later we endeavoured to make out own fairy houses and hid them along a local trail hoping to bring joy to other little fairy-lovers! We stretched our creative minds to turn twigs and bark and leaves into everyday items and architectural masterpieces.

In this project, teens will build a fairy trail. Not only will they get to practice their planning and creating and building skills, they will get the opportunity to give a little magic to some local kids. This project is so much fun that I encourage it to be a family or even a community affair!

GUIDELINES

- **Decide which local nature trail to turn into a fairy trail.** *Being that the houses are made of entirely natural materials, I do not have any concern placing the houses along a trail but you may choose to contact the trail owner for permission.*

- **Decide if the project will be solo or group.** *Your teen can take on all of the designing and building themselves or organize the project to involved family or friends. Doing the trail as a group adds some extra planning skills to the project!*

- **Create a schedule.** *The schedule should include time to design, gather, build, and place the houses. If the project will involve others there will be some communications and meetings on the schedule.*

- **Design houses and household items.** *There are some great books like "Fairy Houses: How to Create Whimsical Homes for Fairy Folk" by Sally Smith that provide designs.*

- **Gather materials.** *And the tools needed to build with.*

- **Build the fairy houses.**

- **Hike out and place the houses along the trail.**

- **Keep it going!** *Even after out initial project was done, we loved making new houses once in a while to add to the trail and we hoped others would too!*

5

Take Over the Kitchen

The best college graduation gift I received was cooking lessons. Eight classes where I learned to chop, saute, and bake. And make a souffle! But even more important than those technical skills were the discussions the instructor had with us around menu planning.

We learned to read recipes and use the information to create a shopping list and a schedule. We talked about planning healthy and delicious meals that met the needs of of families or guests. We got comfortable with keeping en eye to the budget when we were deciding on a menu. We learned not only to cook but to plan a menu.

In this project, teens will create a healthy and delicious meal plan for the week. While this project is definitely complex, teens love it because the results are tangible (they get to eat them!) and they are being given a level of responsibility and control in the household that they may not often get. They may even ask to do this project again!

GUIDELINES

- **Decide on the schedule of meals for the week.** *I give my teens a calendar with Friday take-out and the few on-the-go meals we need for the week. My schedule includes lunch but not breakfast.*
- **Discuss what "healthy" and "delicious" mean in your family.** *In my house we have salad with every meal and at least one vegetable and we might eat dessert once during the week.*
- **Discuss any dietary restrictions.** *We have a vegetarian and a person who is low carb and while we serve one meal to the family, we make sure to provide options for everyone.*
- **Discuss the budget.** *This adds another level of complexity to the project but is essential if there is a weekly food budget and an excellent idea to help all teens make choices and compromises.*
- **Create a meal planner.** *A simple grid with the days of the week on the top and the mealtimes down the side works well. I ask my kids to use a spreadsheet program (for the extra skill building) but paper works just fine.*
- **Explore cookbooks and websites for recipes.**
- **Create a shopping list.** *I make sure my teens understand the layout of the grocery store so that they can organize their list better.*
- **Send your teen shopping.** *Teens can choose to shop solo or if they are newer to the grocery store, go along with a parent to answer any questions.*
- **Prep, cook and serve.** *I like to be on hand in the other room while my teen is cooking a full meal in case they have questions or run across a new technique that they can't learn on YouTube!*
- **Bon appetite!**

6

Create a Stop Motion Animation

My daughters and I recently took a quick online class together in making simple stop motion animations. It was part of the "Lunchtime Creativity" series I created to help my one daughter get over her artist's block.

While I thought it would give us a fun, no-pressure 15 minute art prompt for a few days it turned out to be an activity that we all loved and put a lot of effort into. Our little few second animations took on a life of their own and turned into well-thought out mini-movies.

In this project, teens will create a stop motion animation. While they will have to plan out their story and complete the technical tasks, this project also let's their creativity loose. And the process is so simple that it can easily be done at the kitchen table.

GUIDELINES

- **Come up with a concept for a film.** *This can be the hardest step! If they are really stuck give them a character, a location, and an emotion.*
- **Storyboard the action.** *Stop motion animations can be pretty short and simple, but encourage your teen to create at least six distinct moments in the movie to carry us through the story from beginning to climax to end.*

- **Decide between drawing the animation or using collage pieces.** *Either method is simple. In drawing, your teen will draw each frame, changing the position and expression of characters. In collage, your teen will create parts of the character out of bits of paper and will adjust the bits to change the position and expression of the character. Or they can do a combination of both with perhaps the background drawn and the character a collage.*

- **Download a stop motion app onto their phone.** *We love Stop Motion Studio*

- **Set up a film rig.** *The easiest way to do this is with a few heavy books and a piece of plexiglass. Your teen will stack the books so they are about 6 to 8 inches high then put the plexiglass on with most of it hanging off the side of the stack. Then add another book on top to secure the plexiglass. They will film by placing their phone on the plexiglass and their animation drawing or collage bits under and snap a picture in the app each time they make a change in position.*

- **Add sound effects and music.**

7

Start a Business

When I was a teen I always had an idea for a business. Unfortunately, my parents took my dreams and turned them into reality. The reality that I was just a kid and could not possible start a business.

When my own daughters have come to me with business ideas, I get behind them 100%. I realize that their business will most likely never take off. But isn't that true of most adult businesses? Instead of focusing on success or failure, I focus on learning great life skills like communications and marketing.

In this project, teens will start a business. Any business will do, but a business they love will have a better success rate and be lots more fun! (And try your best not to squash their idea. You may certainly know that nobody is going to be clambering for their lip gloss or their parakeet watching service but nobody knows for sure!)

GUIDELINES

- **Come up with a business idea.**
- **Discuss the things they will need to go in to business.**

1. A product/service idea
2. An elevator pitch
3. A product/service that has been tested
4. Cost and pricing information
5. Start up budget
6. Labeling and packaging (if applicable)
7. Websites or stores to carry their product/service
8. A marketing plan
9. Marketing materials

- **Write up a business plan including all of the items above.** *Teens can find some templates online or just create their own document.*
- **Review the business plan with an advisor.**
- **Find start up capital.**
- **Complete the items in the business plan.** *It might be a good idea to set up a weekly status meeting with your teen to see how they are doing and if they need any adult guidance.*
- **Produce and sell.**

8

Produce a Play

Who doesn't remember putting together a play when they were young? Or at least enjoying watching Jo, Meg, Beth, and Amy do it in "Little Women"? Putting on a play is such a rite of passage!

In this project, teens will produce a short play. Not only will it stretch their artistic brains but it requires amazing amounts of coordination and, even more, negotiation. The play can be a big community affair or just a small family only event!

GUIDELINES

- **Find a script.** *A short script is a good idea or even a few scenes form a longer play. But a long play is great for those who want to tackle it and they can certainly write their own script if they prefer.*
- **Select a date and venue for the performance.** *Be sure teens give themselves enough time and the date does not conflict with anything else important.*
- **Audition and cast the actors.** *It is important to understand each actor's availability for the performance and for rehearsals so be sure to ask!*
- **Create a rehearsal schedule.**
- **Provide actors with the rehearsal schedule and the script.**
- **Hold rehearsals.** *Close to the show there will need to be a dress rehearsal.*

- **Get the word out about the performance.** *If it is just a family affair, a few emails will be good but if it is a community show there will need to be fliers and social media posts.*
- **Get props and costumes.** *Keep props and costumes to things that are readily available or easily made.*
- **Create sets and backdrops.** *Again, this can be kept very simple.*
- **Create a program.**
- **Showtime!**

9

Plan a Trip

My very first planning project was when I was in third grade and I planned a family trip to Washington DC. It was well before the days of the internet and I remember going to the library to check out travel books and get destination addresses in phone books so I could write away for brochures! I picked out all the things we were going to do, scheduled them in during the time frame of our trip, and wrote away for tickets and reservations.

To this day I can still remember how proud I was felt to have curated such an amazing experience (including a tour of the White House) for my family. The trip planning skills I developed in my youth have served me well as I have traveled the world in my adulthood.

In this project, teens will plan a family trip. Planning a big vacation is an extensive project but even planning a day-trip provides teen with the same opportunities to practice those planning skills. It does not matter where you go, just go!

GUIDELINES

- **Select location, time frame, and budget for the trip.** *A trip that is all in one location is easiest but don't be afraid to have them tackle a multi-stop trip.*
- **Talk to everyone in the family about the activities they would like to do.** *Creating a trip that the entire family will enjoy starts with understanding what is important to each family member (great restaurants, no hiking!) and also being clear on absolute must-dos (see the Taj Mahal!) and absolute no-gos (taking a hot-air balloon ride).*
- **Discuss any travel and timing limitations.** *Eager planners may be so excited by all the things to do that they neglect to figure out how long things take and the travel time between them.*
- **Create a planning document for the trip**. *I encourage my teens to use a spreadsheet program (to build those technology skills) but paper works just fine. The document should include dates running down the side and across the top things like location for the day, sleeping arrangements, dining options, things to do, costs and travel time. I suggest a column for notes as well.*
- **Research things to do, sleeping arrangements, and dining options for all the locations you plan to hit and get them scheduled in their planning document.** *Links to websites should be included as well as open days/hours. They should also note cost and travel time between activities and locations.*
- **Review the plan.**
- **Discuss any concerns and revise the plan.** *Keep revising until it works!*
- **Make reservations.** *It is usually a good idea to sit with your teen while they make the reservations. Or at least agree that you get to check the reservation before they hit "confirm".*
- **Bon voyage!**

10

Decorate a Cake

In my previous life, I owned a bakery and created ridiculous cakes that looked life real seagulls and hamburgers and men's hats. My kids loved coming in to watch, and when they got older, help.

Last year they wanted to really learn the skill of cake decorating and did a project that involved designing, baking, and decorating a cake. Such a fun (and delicious) activity gave them the motivation to be not only creative and artistic but really well-organized and determined.

In this project, teens will design, bake, and decorate a cake. They can make one for a special occasion or it's even just really fun to eat a fancy cake on any old Tuesday night.'

GUIDELINES

- **Decide on the style of the cake.** *Cakes are either traditional tiered cakes (like at a wedding) with decorations on the top and the sides or they can be carved (think Ace of Cakes) to look like every day objects.*
- **Design a cake.** *Have your teen grab a book like Debbie Brown's "Magical Cakes", Colette Peters "The Art of Cake Decorating", or Toba Garrett's "Professional Cake Decorating" to get some ideas. Even if they want to decorate*

their's a little differently (different colors or flowers or decorations), it helps to have a general set of instructions to follow so I would not suggest coming up with an entirely custom design.

- **Create a schedule.** *Using the directions for their chosen cake, your teen will create a schedule of when things need to get done based on when they want they cake completed. Shopping needs to be done. Some decorations can or must be made ahead. Cakes need to cool after being baked and rest after being iced. Thoroughly reading the directions is a must!*

- **Go shopping.** *Your teen will be able to find most of the cake and icing ingredients in your local store but some of the decorating items and tools might need to be bought at a craft store or online. NY Cake is my favorite store, in person and online!*

- **Bake the cake and make the filling and icing.**

- **Make decorations.** *If the instructions in the book they are using are not enough, there are plenty of videos on cake decorating techniques on YouTube.*

- **Assemble the cake.**

- **Decorate the cake.**

11

Produce a Magic Show

Every year we attend this really swanky Halloween party with fabulous costumes, a killer DJ, and delicious food but the thing that keeps me coming back year after year is the magician. I could sit there for hours watching his performance with compete and utter amazement.

Not only is learning magic and creating a show a great skill building project, it is also one of those life skills that impresses people later in life at dinner parties and work events!

In this project, teens will learn how to do magic and then create a show to perform for their family, or maybe even the entire community!

GUIDELINES

- **Learn to do magic**. *We love "Penn and Teller Teach the Art of Magic" available on Masterclass. Or they could find some videos online or a book on magic tricks.*
- **Create a magic show.** *Your teen should include tricks they have mastered and script out what they will say to engage the audience in between. They will of course also need an excellent costume and maybe a fabulous assistant!*
- **Practice.** *Practicing for one friend or family member will help your teen to*

perfect their routine and work out their nerves.
- **Schedule a performance.** *Schedule and advertise the performance.*
- **Astound and amaze the audience!**

12

Sew a Costume

I have to admit that I always wanted a packaged Halloween costume. Instead I always got one made by my dad. (That looked way better than anything any of my classmates had.)

I, of course, inherited my dad's penchant for making homemade costumes and did the same for my daughters, who also caught the bug and when they were old enough started making their own. Year after year, it has been a great way to let them practice planning out a project and following instructions with the added bonus of learning to sew!

In this project, teens will sew a Halloween or cosplay costume. Teens will need a sewing machine for this one but they are inexpensive to purchase, or can even be borrowed or rented.

GUIDELINES

- **Head to the fabric store and select a pattern from a pattern book.** *Most pattern books have a costume section and there are even some books dedicated to costumes.*
- **Read the back of the pattern to understand the materials required for the project.** *If your teen is new to sewing, the people who work in the fabric*

store can be a big help explaining how to figure out what they need.

- **Purchase the materials.** *Don't forget the thread! And a good pair of sewing scissors and pins.*
- **Cut out the pattern pieces.** *If your teen is unfamiliar with how to use a pattern, there are plenty of YouTube videos and online classes to help them.*
- **Get basic sewing skills.** *For someone who has never used a sewing machine before, they may want to tackle a simple project, like a tote bag, before they start on their costume. There are plenty of instructions available online.*
- **Sew the costume.** *The pattern will include instructions on how to put everything together. If they mention any new techniques, there are videos available on YouTube to demonstrate them.*

13

Host a Dinner Party

There is something magical about a dinner party. I think it must be turning your little old dining room into a 5-star restaurant.

Putting together a dinner party takes the creativity of an artist and the precision of a Marine. That might also be what makes is so magical!

In this project, teens will plan and execute a dinner party. It could be for their own friends or for yours. I am not sure which one is less stressful, but careful planning makes the evening flow much easier!

GUIDELINES

- **Decide who will be coming to the dinner party.** *If your teen is new to this sort of thing, pick some family members or close friends that won't mind if things don't go perfectly.*
- **Discuss a date and theme for the party.** *A date that is not too close to anything else major is important. The theme can be a season, a style of food, or even something fun and silly.*
- **Discuss any restrictions for the party.** *There may be a few food requirements or allergies.*
- **Plan the menu.** *I suggest some appetizers while people are arriving then a*

soup and/or salad course, an entree, and a dessert. It is a good idea to have only a couple of items that need last minute attention.

- **Plan the table setting.** *Using the dishes, tablecloths and napkins you already have is a good idea. But your teen can customize the table with candles, a centerpiece, and a few other decorative items.*
- **Create a schedule.** *Teens will need to schedule some tasks ahead of time and some the day of. The ahead of time tasks can just be placed on a day, but the last minute tasks will need to be planned down to the minute in order for everything to run smoothly.*
- **Review the schedule.** *A little guidance from a seasoned cook is helpful to insure that the timing works well.*
- **Make a shopping list.**
- **Go shopping.**
- **Set the table and prep the food.**
- **Serve and clear.** *But maybe offer to do the dishes for your teen after the party!*

14

Redecorate a Room

It feels like every summer for the past five years, one or both of my daughters have wanted to redecorate their room. But after one big change for each of them from "little girl" to "teen", I was not really up for the task.

So I let them do it. Armed with a small a budget and a lot of freedom, they managed their redecoration projects like seasoned HGTV hosts! They knew that I was not going to push to have the project done and if they wanted something fresh they were going to have to do the work and stick to the plan.

In this project, teens will redecorate a room. Most likely their own! This is a big project but a teen can and will handle it on their own. I promise!

GUIDELINES

- **Discuss the budget.** *We have ranged from $100 for a little refresh to $1000 for a whole new room.*
- **Discuss any limitations.** *Perhaps painting is out. Maybe an heirloom dresser can't be touched. Holes in the walls might be a no-no. Make the constraints clear!*
- **Create a scale plan.** *Teens can do it on paper or using apps like "Plan Your Room" or "Room Sketcher". They will have to measure their room and their*

existing furniture and get it all laid out.

- **Design their new room.** *Using their scale plan, they can rearrange or replace furniture and make notes of color changes and accessory changes.*
- **Create a vision board.** *Have your teen print out the new items they want, along with the scale plan, and color swatches and place them on a poster board. Prices of new items should be included as well.*
- **Discuss the design.** *Before any work can be done, your teen will present their vision board. This is the time to veto, suggest, and praise!*
- **Create a schedule.** *Nobody wants a drawn out renovation so teens need to figure out what steps need to get done, in what order.*
- **Go shopping or order new items online.** *Be sure to stick to the budget!*
- **Tackle the painting, assembly and decorating.**

15

Build a Gingerbread House

Every year I build a gingerbread house. I have made replicas of my own house and of the Pyramids of Giza. I have created beach bungalows and the Eiffel Tower. Once there was even a Lenni Lenape longhouse. And every year my daughters have helped.

By making gingerbread houses with me they learned to to bake and to decorate. But they also learned to do the geometry and measuring required for building, they have explored architectural styles, and they learned to be good problem solvers because building a house out of cake is a giant mistake waiting to happen!

In this project, teens will build a gingerbread house. In addition to all of the planning skills required to go from bowl of flour and molasses to work of art, they will most definitely learn a bit of resilience and patience! This project is one that makes a bit of a mess so be prepared. But I can guarantee that the result will be magical!

GUIDELINES

- **Pick a house design.** *I highly suggest getting a book like "The Gingerbread Architect" by Susan Matheson or "The Gingerbread Book" by Allen Bragdon that has ready made plans unless your teen has advanced math or architecture skills.*
- **Create a shopping list.** *Not only will they need the gingerbread and icing ingredients they may need some basic decorating supplies and tools. They will need to thoroughly read the instructions to understand what these things might be.*
- **Create a paper template.** *Even if your teen is using a design from a book, they will need to recreate a full scale template on paper.*
- **Bake the gingerbread pieces.**
- **Make the icing.**
- **Build the house.** *Remind your teen that this is where a little problem solving might come in! Rarely do the pieces of the house fit together perfectly. They will need to use supports (like cans of soup) or maybe a second set of hands or sometimes a few pins. They will have to wait for things to dry and perhaps revise their decoration plan to cover up some problem areas.*
- **Decorate the house.** *While your teen can decorate the house exactly as instructed in the book, they can also let their creativity blossom by changing it up and making it their own.*

16

Plant a Garden

As a teen, I remember the very first carrot I grew. I remember plucking it from the ground, brushing the dirt off and eating it down to the leaves right there in the garden. I will admit that that carrot was pretty much the only thing I have ever been able to grow, but I have never stopped trying.

While my garden today may be mostly easy-to-grow herbs and some cherry tomatoes in a pot, encouraging my teens to experiment with growing their own food is important to me. Even if it is only enough to make a small side salad!

In this project, teens will build start a garden. A full outdoor garden or just a few windowsill pots just to get started are both totally great gardens!

GUIDELINES

- **Discuss where the garden will be.**
- **Research items to grow.** *Your teen will need to understand what each plant needs in terms of light and space and be sure they have that in their garden.*
- **Learn about planting and caring for each item in the garden.** *"Gardening for Dummies" is a great place to start.*
- **Purchase plants or seeds.** *It is more expensive to purchase plants but may*

prove easier for the first time gardener.

- **Purchase any soil, food, and fertilizer that is needed.**
- **Plant the garden.** *Teens must be aware that planting seeds usually happens indoors in the very early spring so they must plan for that!*
- **Tend to the garden.**
- **Harvest and enjoy!**

17

Cook an Entire Cookbook

Did you ever see the movie "Julie & Julia"? It was the true story of writer Julie Powell who decided to cook the entire contents of Julia Child's "Mastering the Art of French Cooking" and blog about it. I always loved Julie's hero's journey but I was mostly just a little jealous that she had thought of such a fabulous idea! So eventually I borrowed the idea and started cooking my way through one of Thomas Keller's cookbooks!

Not only did I up my cooking game, but I learned to power through some difficult situations that I would rather have avoided. Like Julie when she had to tackle the recipe where she de-boned a duck. I learned that sometimes there are obstacles that we just need to get through in order to reach out goal and that in the end they usually turn out to be a mild discomfort and not a huge trauma!

In this project, teens will cook the contents of an entire cookbook. They will gain not only new cooking skills but a great sense of accomplishment. This project is a big one but it can be managed by the size and complexity of the cookbook and the time-frame for completion. And just think of all of the amazing things you are going to get to eat!

GUIDELINES

- **Select a cookbook.** *Your teen's comfort level in the kitchen and enthusiasm for this project will guide them to a good choice. Picking a cookbook too large and complicated is not a good recipe for success.*
- **Discuss the time-frame.** *Will they be cooking each day and wrap up in a month? Or cook once a week and take an entire year?*
- **Create a schedule of when they will tackle each recipe.**
- **Think about creating a blog or vlog or Instagram account to track progress.** *Sometimes being accountable to your audience gives you the extra motivation you need to get past some tough spots.*
- **Create a weekly shopping list.** *And go shopping.*
- **Thoroughly read each recipe before making it to be sure they are prepared with tools, techniques, and ingredients.** *Be sure your teen gets clarification on any techniques that are new to them. You Tube has loads of great cooking technique videos.*
- **Cook the masterpieces.** *I like to hang around in the next room while my teens tackle new recipes in case they have questions!*
- **Snap some food photos and enjoy!**

18

Invest in the Stock Market

When I was in high school, as part of our math class we each pretended to invest in the stock market. We were given an amount of "money" and we picked the stocks we wanted to invest in. Then we charted their progress each day and decided if we wanted to buy or sell. Everyone was so into it that we almost forgot it was not real money!

I did the same project with my homeschooled teens. But I gave them real money to invest. You can open an account for your teen for as little as $500.

In this project, teens will invest in the stock market. It is not only a great project but a great investment in their financial future.

GUIDELINES

- **Discuss the stock market.** *Give them a brief overview of how it works.*
- **Open a brokerage account.** *eTrade is a great option. Or they can make purchases in your stock account. Or you can set up a faux account!*
- **Decide how much to invest.** *This can be money you give them, savings they have, or faux money.*
- **Learn about investing.** *There are some great books like "Investing for Dummies" by Eric Tyson, "Buffettology" by Mary Buffett, and "Teenvestor"*

by Emmanuel Modo.

- **Buy some stocks.**
- **Check in every once in a while on the stocks and make decisions about buying new shares or selling some.** *Let them make their own choices. It is the best way to learn.*

19

Create an Historical Cookbook

Every time we study history, my daughters insist that we make lunch from that period almost every day.

There is something really fun about trying recipes that were invented centuries ago. Learning about ingredients, techniques, and dining styles from the past is a great way to learn about ancient cultures and our ancestors.

In this project, teens will create a cookbook of historical recipes. They can choose to cover all of history, the history of a particular country or region, or a certain time period.

GUIDELINES

- **Pick a location and/or a time period.**
- **Find recipes from their location and time period.**
- **Research unusual ingredients, techniques or tools by doing additional research.**
- **Rewrite each recipe, explaining the ingredients, techniques and tools and what substitutions we can make today.** *It is one thing to just copy and paste someone's recipe into your cookbook but another thing to truly understand the recipe and guide others to use it.*

- **Make the recipes and take photos.** *Teens can take a photo of the final product or perhaps some of the ingredients or a few of the process.*
- **Compile the recipes into a cookbook.** *Teens can create a paper cookbook or create a blog full of the recipes instead so that others can find and use them.*
- **Add a little context or story before sharing the recipe.** *Giving the reader a feel for when this dish might have been served or how it was created adds a lot of value.*

20

Start a Teen Magazine

A few weeks ago a woman I know was telling me all about how her teen started a magazine. I immediately added this to the list of things I want to give my teens the opportunity to do!

The magazine my friend's daughter started was devoted to the arts and included works from local teen artists, poets, writers, photographers, comics, and more. It is published online quarterly and has been a great gathering place for local teens.

In this project, teens will publish a magazine by teens, for teens.

GUIDELINES

- **Come up with an idea for a magazine.** *Art, fashion, science, religion, anything they are passionate about.*
- **Decide if they are going to lead the entire magazine or gather a group to run it.**
- **Figure out the logistics of the magazine.** *Will it be paper or online? (Blurb is a great website to publish paper magazines.) How often will it be published? What types of content will be in the magazine? What will the name be?*
- **Contact friends, relatives, and the community to ask for submissions.**

Be sure to provide a deadline!

- **Create a format for the magazine.** *Lucidpress is a great platform for formatting a magazine or it can be done in Google Docs or even as a website.*
- **Lay out the magazine with all of the submissions.**
- **Publish the magazine and get the word out that it exists!** *Be sure readers know how they can submit to the next edition!*

21

Publish a Children's Book

When I was younger I wrote an amazing children's book, "Lizzie the Ladybug" and it is still in my local elementary school library for kids to take out and enjoy.

In this project, teens will write and illustrate a children's book. Writing a children's book is a great opportunity for teens to flex their creative muscles in a really fun way.

GUIDELINES

- **Come up with an idea for a book.** *Teens should have a list of a couple of characters and an introduction, a conflict, a climax, and a resolution.*
- **Write the story.** *Keep in mind that children's books usually only have a few lines on a page!*
- **Illustrate the book.** *Artists will love drawing their own artwork. Other teens can get a friend to illustrate or get creative and use stick figures, collage, photographs or anything else that provide a visual element.*
- **Have someone edit and proofread.**
- **Publish the book.** *Teens can publish your book at Kindle Direct Publishing for free! And even order discount copies to bring to local stores to sell.*

22

Organize a Charity Scavenger Hunt

My daughters and I recently did this crazy global scavenger hunt. We joined a team from all of the world online and spent the weekend making portraits out of the trash, having ugly sweater meetings, feeding each other with a six foot long spoon, and more.

We had such a fun time that we thought it would be a great idea for our local community. And having the kids plan it would be a great project.

In this project, teens will create and organize a scavenger hunt. Not only will they have to come up with ideas but they will have to manage the hunt like a mini-business to be sure it runs smoothly.

GUIDELINES

- **Figure out the logistics of the hunt.** *They will need to think through a date, the location, how teams will be formed, how signups will happen, how the list will be distributed, how the hunt will be scored., and what the winner gets They may also want to do the scavenger hunt as a charity fundraiser and charge for participation.*
- **Approach the town, if you feel approval will be needed.**
- **Create an ad for the hunt.** *Flyers can be posted around town, emails can be*

sent, and or social media posts can be made.
- **Manage sign ups.** *They may want to use a sign up app like Sign Up Genius or just take signups by email.*
- **Create some rules to keep everyone safe.**
- **Create a list of the scavenger hunt items.**
- **Create instructions to let hunters know how to submit items.**
- **Send a reminder to everyone who signed up a few days before.**
- **Start the hunt.**
- **Score the submissions and announce the winner!**

23

Create a Coffee Table Book

After a trip to Italy a few years ago, we returned home with a collection of hundreds of pictures. Not of us. Not of famous landmarks. Of cats. Hundreds of pictures of cats. I jokingly suggested we create a coffee table book called "The Gattos of Italy".

A coffee table book is a fun way to do something with all those pictures your teen has of that random thing that interests them. Or it can serve as the inspiration to get out and take pictures of the random thing that interests them.

In this project, teens will create coffee table book based on something they love. it can be just for your table or also makes a really great gift.

GUIDELINES

- **Pick a topic.**
- **Take (more) photographs.**
- **Learn a bit about photography to capture some more advanced shots.**
- **Format the book.** *The easiest option is to use a photo service like Snapfish or Shutterfly.*
- **Add an introduction to the book and to give some information (like**

location or subject matter) for each photo.

· **Print and share.**

24

Organize a Flash Mob

Flash mobs are surprise gatherings of people who briefly perform a dance or other entertaining act. They are really fun to participate in. I mean, who doesn't love to be part of a secret? And they are definitely put a little surprise into the day of anyone who gets to watch.

In this project, teens will organize a flash mob of their friends.

GUIDELINES

- **Choreograph a dance (or find a friend who can do it).** *Keep it simple so dancers and non-dancers can all participate.*
- **Recruit a number of friends for the mob.** *Remind them to keep quiet about it!*
- **Meet with the mob to decide when and where to flash.**
- **Teach the mob the choreography and rehearse together at least once.** *If it is hard to get together, your teen can record themselves teaching the dance and send everyone the video.*
- **Organize someone to play the music and record the event.**

25

Throw a Surprise Party

Is there anyone out there who doesn't love a surprise party? (Well, my mother.) Throwing a surprise party can be as much fun for the organizers as it is for the birthday guy or gal.

In this project, teens will plan and throw a surprise party for a friend. You don't even have to wait for their birthday, just throw them a party just for fun!

GUIDELINES

- **Pick a good friend (or family member) having a special day in the next few months.**
- **Form a planning committee of a few people close to the birthday guy or gal.** *This is a great way to learn to be a leader instead of doing all the work themselves.*
- **Decide on a date, theme, location, guest list, dress code, invites, food, cake, decorations, music, entertainment, how the birthday guy or gal will get there, etc.** *Your teen will need to take into account any budget.*
- **Have the committee divide up work and set deadlines.** *Your teen will also want to set up another meeting to make sure everything is happening.*
- **Make sure that invites go out, that all purchases are made by the day before the party, and that everything gets set up the day of the party.**

26

Design a Board Game

My teens were often jealous when they heard the howling laughter coming from downstairs where the adults were playing "Cards Against Humanity" after dinner parties. So one year, for Christmas, I made them "Cards Against Christmas". It was a very PG-rated, holiday-themed version of the game that I wrote up and had printed on playing cards. It was a hit and has inspired other board game creation in our household.

In this project, teens will design their own board game. They can create it out of poster board and markers or look for online sites that turn their ideas into real games.

GUIDELINES

- **Come up with a theme for the board game.** *It could be based on a sport or a book or a love of travel or math*
- **Decide on the objective of the game.** *Find the hidden treasure? Survive the apocalypse? Eat the most Twinkies?*
- **Think through the mechanics of the game.** *Will they use dice or a spinner to move ahead? Are there cards that cause things to happen? Is there money or points involved?*
- **Come up with the rules.**

- **Design and make the game board and pieces.**
- **Have family game night!**

27

Teach a Class

The best way to become a master at something is to teach it to someone else. It is called the "protege effect". Teaching someone else requires you to organize what you know, increases your motivation to learn, and brings your knowledge to a new depth.

In the project, teens will prepare and teach a class in something they love. They can pick something they know and love or something they love and are learning about!

GUIDELINES

- **Pick a topic.**
- **Decide where they will teach the lesson, make contact with the organization, and set a date.** *Local libraries or community centers are great places for teens to offer their services.*
- **Organize what they are going to teach.** *Creating an outline of the class is a great idea.*
- **Collect any materials or create any presentations they will need.**
- **Practice the presentation points and demonstrations.**
- **Let the participants know if they need anything for class.** *Workout clothes, a notebook etc.*

28

Build a Mini Golf Course

I might have been a strange kid but every time I went mini-golfing, I was less interested in my score and more interested in imagining what my own mini-golf course would look like!

I never got to create one but it filled my dreams enough times that I feel like I did. The design and the building and the grand opening! It would have been a pretty cool thing.

In this project, teens will design and build their own mini-golf course. It's a pretty epic project! And yes, it requires a lot of space and some decent building skills. But if they don't have those things it might even be better because they will need to figure them out!

GUIDELINES

- **Select a space.** *Your teen may have a large enough yard to fit a few holes. Or they might need to reach out to their community to borrow a space or create a movable min-golf course that can be set up and taken away!*
- **Decide the theme of the golf course and how many holes it will be.**
- **Design each hole.** *There are plenty of ideas out on the internet or take a trip to a local course to do some research. Each hole will need to have a shape, a*

terrain, and an obstacle in the theme.

- **Create a building schedule and a budget.** *Once they have a design, they can figure out if they can build it.*
- **Revise the design.** *Based on schedule and budget constraints, some design changes may need to happen.*
- **Put together a materials list.**
- **Go shopping.**
- **Build each hole**. *Unless your teen is used to building, they may need some assistance with power tools!*
- **Paint and decorate each hole.**

II

Building Activities

Building things is all about following instructions. Or creating your own.

The projects in this section will not only help your teen learn to follow directions but will also help them build the determination and creativity necessary to adjust when the instructions might not work out as expected.

29

Make a Water Clock

The clepsydra, or water clock, was a valuable time tracking tool in ancient times. It used the flow of water to track time and was first thought to have been used in Greece around 325 BC to time speeches made in courts of law.

Teens can make their own simple water clock using only a plastic bottle or make a more permanent water clock with some clay or plastic pots.

INSTRUCTIONS FOR A SIMPLE WATER CLOCK

- Collect a plastic water bottle and a pair of scissors.
- Cut a plastic bottle in half. The top should be slightly shorter than the bottom. *The bigger the bottle, the longer amount of time you can track.*
- Puncture the lid with a hole approximately 1/8 inch in size.
- Place the lid back on the bottle.
- Place the top of the bottle, upside down, inside the bottom of the bottle. *The lid should be about 4 inches from the bottom.*
- Pour water into the top of the bottle and mark the water level in the bottom of the bottle after 1 minute, 2 minutes, 3 minutes, etc.
- Now use the water clock to tell how much time has passed!

INSTRUCTIONS FOR AN ADVANCED WATER CLOCK

- **Collect 2 large containers, a wooden dowel, a wine cork, 2 eyelet screws, and a wooden stake.**
- **Follow these instructions from WikiHow** https://www.wikihow.com/Make-a-Water-Clock-(Clepsydra)#Advanced-Water-Clock

30

Build a Paper Automata

An automata is a machine that performs a function according to a predetermined set of coded instructions. Turn the crank and watch the cat jump up and down! They are a great way to explore cams, levers, and linkages while creating a moving piece of art.

Teens can make an automata using cardboard and paper scraps and a few items found in the junk drawer or create more complex automata from books like "Paper Automata" by Rob Ives or kits on Etsy.

INSTRUCTIONS FOR A SIMPLE AUTOMATA

- **Gather up a cardboard box, some foam pieces, pipe cleaners, straws, scissors, and a glue gun.**
- **Follow these instructions from Exploratorium** automata. https://www.exploratorium.edu/pie/downloads/Cardboard_Automata.pdf

31

Make Wine

Wine making might seem like an odd project for a teen, but they are making it, not drinking it! It is a great science experiment and a cool skill to have for the future.

Teens can make wine from any fruit juice!

INSTRUCTIONS FOR MAKING WINE

- **You will need fruit juice, sugar, yeast, and tannins.**
- **Making wine is a bit like science so following detailed instructions is important!** *You can look online or grab a copy of "Winemaking for Dummies".*

32

Build a Model Boat or Plane

When I was a kid, model building was a big thing. Everyone always seemed to be working on a boat or plane or out buying those little jars of really smelly paint!

Teens can make a model as a simple, cardboard model or head to the hobby store and select an age-appropriate model .

INSTRUCTIONS FOR BUILDING A CARDBOARD MODEL

- **Collect cereal boxes, hot glue gun, scissors, and a ruler.**
- **Follow the instructions from Instructables** https://www.instructables.com/id/Easy-Cardboard-Model-Airplane/

33

Make a Solar Cell Phone Charger

Nobody likes their phone to run out of battery. Especially not teens. Which is why they love building their own cell phone charger.

Teens can build a cell phone charger out of an Altoids tin and a few inexpensive electrical components.

INSTRUCTIONS FOR BUILDING A SOLAR CELL PHONE CHARGER

- **Find an empty Altoid container, a 4V or greater solar cell AA or AAA battery holder, a 1N914 Blocking Diode, electrical tape and a soldering iron**
- **Look up the instructions for "Solar Charger" in the Brown Dog Gadgets blog.**

34

Make a Sundial

A sundial is simply a device that tells the time of day based on the sun's position in the sky.

Teen's can make their own sundial with things as simple as a stick and some rocks or create a more permanent sundial using a large wood or stone disk as the base and painting on the numbers.

INSTRUCTIONS FOR A SUNDIAL

- **Find a sunny spot of grass. The spot has to get sun all day long!** *To complete the sundial in one day, start early!*
- **Find a 2 foot long straight stick and push it into the earth.** *If you are in the Northern hemisphere, point it slightly north. In the Southern, south.*
- **On the hour, place a rock on the shadow from the stick.** *Painting the hour on the rock can be a good idea.*
- **Return each hour to place a new rock.**
- **Continue until there are 12 rocks around the stick.**

35

Build a Model House

Everyone is fascinated by those little paper model buildings you find in museums or at architects offices. You can't help but picture yourself wandering through!

Teens can make a model house of their own home or a personal design. A simple house can be made out of cardboard from the recycling bin or you can purchase "3-D Home Kit" online for about $30.

INSTRUCTIONS FOR BUILDING A MODEL HOUSE

- **Collect a tissue box, scrap cardboard/ cardboard boxes, printer paper, glue, a ruler, an X-Acto knife, and scissors.**
- **Follow the instructions from Instructables** https://www.instructables.com/id/Build-a-Model-Cardboard-House/

36

Build a Tipi

I never felt the need for a big backyard. Until I saw those amazing backyard tipis where you could flop onto a pile of pillows and read the summer day away. While we couldn't have one in our yard, we did undertake building one in the woods once. It definitely tested our engineering skills. And our patience!

Teens can build their own backyard tipi using just nine poles and a dropcloth. Painting the drop cloth adds an extra level of art to the tipi.

INSTRUCTIONS FOR BUILDING A TIPI

- Gather nine 10 foot poles (1 to 1.25 inches in diameter, a 12 x 15 canvas drop cloth, rope, string, a tape measure, scissors, and a marker.
- Gather three of the poles together and wrap rope around it several times about 1 1/2 feet from the end. Tie a tight double knot at the end and trim the excess.
- In the middle of the space, stand the 3 tied poles in the middle with the rope at the top. Spread the three poles out, like a tripod, to the diameter you want your tipi base.
- Lay the remaining poles between the three that are tied, with the bottoms forming the base circle of the tipi.
- Lay the canvas flat and mark the center of the long edge.

- Tie one end of a string to the marker. Place the marker at one end of the longest edge of the canvas. Stretch the string to the center mark. Extend it a couple of inches longer and cut the string. Have someone hold the string in place on the center mark and draw a large semi-circle beginning at one end of the longest edge and finishing at the opposite end.
- Cut on the semicircle.
- Cut 12 strips from the remaining canvas, 1.5 inches by 18 inches.
- Wrap the canvas around the pole structure with the straight edge at the top and semi-circle at the bottom. Begin by placing the center mark on the canvas at the top of the pole in the back, opposite of where the door will be.
- Cut two slits about 1 1/2 inches apart at the top where the two sides of the canvas meet. Tie the two sides of the canvas together with one of the strips threaded through the two holes and tied and knotted. Picture this like putting on a cape and tying it at the neck!
- Cut two more slits halfway down the sides of the opening. Use another strip to tie this together when you want the door closed.
- For added support, cut slits at the bottom on either side of the poles and tie canvas to poles with canvas strips.

37

Design a House

My daughters and I love driving around looking at houses. And we love designing our own just for fun.

Teens can play architect by creating plans for houses by drawing them or using simple online software, SketchUp.

INSTRUCTIONS FOR DRAFTING A HOUSE PLAN

- **Grab some graph paper and a scale ruler.**
- **Follow the instructions from Instructables** https://www.instructables.com/id/How-to-Manually-Draft-a-Basic-Floor-Plan/

38

Build a Lego Landmark

I'm sorry, but you are never too old for Legos! Your teen may balk at the idea of "playing" with Legos but I promise that if you can get them over the "coolness" factor, they will be re-hooked!

Teens can build various world landmarks out of Legos using online instructions or grab the book "Style and Structure Volume 1: Lego Building Instructions for World Landmarks" by Jennifer Kemmeter.

INSTRUCTIONS FOR BUILDING A LEGO LANDMARK

- **Pull out all your old Legos.**
- **Head over to Brick Instructions for instructions on various landmarks** https://lego.brickinstructions.com/en/lego_instructions/theme/lego_architecture

39

Make a Dream Catcher

A dream catcher is a beautiful talisman that is hung over your bed and is said to catch your bad dreams. It is made of a hoop with a web woven in the center and beads and feathers hanging from the bottom.

Teens can make a dream catcher with a few supplies found in the craft store, or even around the house.

INSTRUCTIONS FOR MAKING A DREAM CATCHER

- **Gather a hoop (an embroidery hoop works well), thin ribbon, string (embroidery floss works well), beads, and feathers.**
- **Start by gluing down one end of the lace to the hoop. Wrap the hoop with the ribbon, until it is completely covered. Glue again at the end.**
- **Cut a piece of string 10 times the diameter of your hoop.**
- **Tie one end of the string securely to the hoop.**
- **To weave the web, I highly suggest watching a video like "Learn to Make a Dreamcatcher Web" by Gloria Chan on YouTube.**
- **Tie a loop of lace at the top for hanging.**
- **Decorate the dream catcher by hanging feathers and beads from the bottom.**

40

Build a Rube Goldberg Machine

Have you ever seen OK Go's video for "This Too Shall Pass"? The song is catchy but what is amazing is the giant Rube Goldberg machine they built for the video. A Rube Goldberg machine, named after American cartoonist Rube Goldberg, is a machine intentionally designed to perform a simple task in an indirect and overly complicated way. Think of that old game "Mousetrap". Watching a Rube Goldberg work is amazing but creating your own is really fun too.

Teens can build a Rube Goldberg machine with items they find around the house.

INSTRUCTIONS FOR CREATING A RUBE GOLDBERG MACHINE

- **There are none! Just play and build!** (*Okay, a working knowledge of levers, pulleys, ramps and screws is helpful!*)

41

Make Syrup

For us city kids there is really nothing more magical than making our own maple syrup! Harvesting something from a neighborhood tree and one day putting it over your waffles is is kind of mind-blowing.

Teens can make syrup from any sap-producing tree.

INSTRUCTIONS FOR MAKING SYRUP

- **Purchase a tree tapping kit.** *You can buy a complete kit online or create one with items from the hardware store.*
- **Go on the hunt for a maple tree and tap it according to the instructions.**
- **Turn the sap into syrup by boiling it until it thickens and reaches 219 degrees.** *This is best done OUTSIDE as it creates a lot of steam!*

42

Make Homemade Paper

Homemade paper is not exactly the paper we are used to. It sort of like a loaf of artisan sourdough bread compared to the bagged grocery store white bread. Special. And really fun to make.

Teens can make paper out of any paper you have in the recycling bin, an old window screen, and an old picture frame.

INSTRUCTIONS FOR MAKING PAPER

- **You will need scrap paper, a blender, an old screen, and a picture frame.**
- **Tear up your paper into small bits.**
- **Blend the paper in the blender with about 2 times as much water as paper until it is the consistency of thick soup.**
- **Place the screen on top of a washtub or slop sink and place the frame on top.**
- **Pour the paper pulp into the frame and the spread with a spatula, being careful not to press too hard.**
- **Remove the frame and cover the pulp with a piece of felt.**
- **Use a sponge to press on top of the felt and help the water drain.**
- **When there is no more water draining, remove the felt and place the paper somewhere to dry.**

43

Build a Terrarium

Terrariums are simple little gardens build in glass jars. Perfect for teens. Or anyone who kills plants when they look at them.

Teens can make a terrarium with a glass jar and a few items from the garden center.

INSTRUCTIONS FOR MAKING A TERRARIUM

- **Collect a glass container (from a pickle jar to an antique urn), rocks (or pebbles, shells, glass marbles), sheet moss, soil, and a few plants that won't grow too much.**
- **Place the rocks at the bottom for drainage.** *The bigger the jar, the more rocks needed.*
- **Soak the moss in water for a few seconds then squeeze out any excess liquid. Place the moss on the rocks, covering them entirely so that no soil can fall through.**
- **Place a layer of soil on top of the moss.**
- **Plant the plants in the soil. Add extra soil to cover the roots and tamp down.**
- **Give the terrarium a good water.** *Keep in mind it only drains through to the rocks so be mindful of over-watering!*

- **Add some decorative items around the plants like other rocks or little figures.**

44

Build a Lamp

Lamps are pretty darn functional. But when you make your own it can also be entirely YOU!

Teens can design and build their own lamp out of household items and a few things from the electrical department.

INSTRUCTIONS FOR BUILDING A LAMP

- **You will need to find something to use as a lamp base and a lamp kit.**
- **Build your own lamp with these simple instructions from WikiHow** https://www.wikihow.com/Build-a-Lamp

III

Kindness Activities

Kindness Activities encourage teens to express kindness to themselves and others.

The projects in this section will help your teen to deepen their relationship with themselves and to broaden their relationship with the world.

45

Send a Care Package

Few things are more exciting than getting a care package. It might have been my favorite part of college, in fact! So I can image what an uplifting feeling it must be to receive one when circumstances are not ideal.

GUIDELINES

- **Pick an organization that gets care packages to people.** *AnySoldier.com helps get care packages to active duty soldiers and OperationRefugeeChild.org helps get care packages to Syrian refugees and BlessingBagBrigadeNJ.org helps get care packages to the homeless.*
- **Think of items that would be useful and items that would inspire joy and fun.** *Some organizations have lists of things they would like included or things that should not be included.*
- **Shop, package, and send.**

46

Do a Cleanup

We are blessed to have so many beautiful places on this planet to enjoy including trails, parks, and beaches. Teens can do their part by keeping them clean and healthy for generations to enjoy.

GUIDELINES

- Look for a group that does cleanups or just head out alone.
- Encourage your teen to dress to protect against poison ivy and to bring cloves to protect against sharp objects.
- Have bags to collect trash and pruning sheets if there is going to do any clipping.

47

Random Acts of Kindness

Doing nice things for no reason is a great habit to start early. A "Random Acts of Kindness Challenge" is a great way to practice this skill.

GUIDELINES

- **Use a 30 day challenge list.** *You can create your own, look one up online, or use the one provided below.*
- **Pick a new act every day for a month.**

RANDOM ACTS OF KINDNESS

1. Leave a positive note in a coffee shop.
2. Pick a friend and celebrate them all day like its their birthday.
3. Compliment a stranger.
4. Pick a small business and leave a positive review online.
5. Hold the door for someone.
6. Leave a positive note in a library book.
7. Offer to babysit for free one night.
8. Make dinner for your family.
9. Leave double your normal tip.

10. Write positive messages around town in sidewalk chalk.
11. Leave change in a vending machine.
12. Let someone ahead of you in line.
13. Feed the birds.
14. Buy a drink for the person in line behind you.
15. Call an older relative.
16. Leave a gift in the mailbox for the mail carrier.
17. Give a copy of a favorite book to someone who might like it.
18. Paint rocks with motivational words and leave them around town.
19. Take in a neighbors garbage cans.
20. Offer to walk someones dog for them.
21. Bake cookies for a friend.
22. Pick up litter.
23. Say "thank you".
24. Donate outgrown clothes.
25. Buy a lottery ticket and leave it on someone's windshield.
26. Say "hello" to everyone you pass on the street.
27. Give someone a hug.
28. Volunteer.
29. Send a postcard to a relative or friend.
30. Make an inspirational social media post.

48

Refashion Clothing

Refashioning was a big craze a few years ago and while it has fallen out of favor, it is still a project that is fun and reminds teens that we don't just have to throw things away, we can make them in to something new.

GUIDELINES

- **Pick a few items of clothing destined for the trash.**
- **Search the internet for interesting refashioning projects.** *T-shirts seem to be the easiest.*
- **Cut, paint, tie, and sew until they have a few new items.** *And a few less for the trashcan.*

49

Create a Vision Board

A vision board is a collage of images, pictures, and affirmations of one's dreams and desires, designed to provide inspiration and motivation.

GUIDELINES

- **Decide on a goal to realize.** *It can be a general "what I want life to look like in 5 years" or it can be a specific "my goal is to get a dog".*
- **Collect images of things that support the goal.** *Pictures can be ones they took, drawings they made, from a magazine or printed from online.*
- **Create a board that includes their images along with any inspirational words or quotes.** *They can do this on a poster board or in an online collage.*
- **Post the vision board where it can be seen each day.**

50

Organize a Charity Drive

Charity drives are an important way to help both people and earth by taking items destined for the trash and giving them a new home with someone who will appreciate them.

GUIDELINES

- **Pick an organization to collect for.** *It can be as simple as your local food pantry or as random as collecting used dance costumes for Traveling Tutus. There seem to be a place for everything!*
- **Create a flyer or social media post for their drive.** *The ad should provide the dates for the drive, the organization being supported, what goods are being collected, and where to drop them off. Some organizations already have marketing materials to use.*
- **Collect and donate.**

51

Write Morning Pages

One of my all-time favorite books is "The Artist's Way" by Julia Cameron. And my favorite practice, which I still do today after reading the book over 20 years ago, is morning pages. It is a great way to get all of your "stuff out before you start your day.

GUIDELINES

- **Grab a plain old notebook.**
- **Write 3 pages first thing in the morning.** *These are just for them. Nobody else will see. They can be about anything. Some days they are about something that happened and others about a problem trying to sort itself out and some days about nothing at all.*
- **Fill all 3 pages!** *Don't give up even if it means writing "I have nothing to write" for two and a half pages before something comes out. I promise something almost always does!*
- **Remember that there is no end result here!** *This is just all about the process of observing what is in your own mind and letting it be free.*

52

Do A Flea Market Flip

My daughters and I love watching "Flea Market Flip" and seeing people turn scary, horrible things they found in someone's Grandma's basement into something we would love to have in our house. We have done our own version a few times, and not only is it fun but it a provides a great feeling of accomplishment from creating something out of nothing and putting one less item into the landfill.

GUIDELINES

- Head to a flea market, antique store, or even the basement.
- Select an item to redesign and rebuild.
- Using tools and materials around the house, turn the item into something new and beautiful.

53

Volunteer

Volunteering not only helps those you are working for but also yourself. Volunteering has been proven to increase self-confidence, sense of purpose, and happiness in the volunteer.

GUIDELINES

- **Pick an organization that is meaningful.** *We are so much more passionate and do a much better job when it is something we care about.*
- **Agree to volunteer one time or on a regular, ongoing basis.**

54

Create a Time Capsule

Creating a time capsule allows us to be here in the present, looking at what is important to us at this moment in time. But it also inspires us to look towards the future and wonder what we will be like when we open the capsule in 10 or 20 years. And we also can't help but be guided to look to the past and how we have grown as we do this exercise.

GUIDELINES

- **Decide on the audience for the time capsule. Future self? Future generations? Total strangers?** *The audience will influence what goes into the capsule.*
- **Collect items for the time capsule.** *There can be personal items, news clippings, photographs, anything that tells the story of everyday life today.*
- **Write a letter to include in the capsule.**
- **Pack the capsule in a container that will keep things dry and protected.**
- **Write the "open on" date on the capsule.** *If the capsule is for strangers to find, they should write that on the container.*
- **Bury the container underground or hide in somewhere in the house.**

55

Start a Meditation Practice

Most teens run screaming the other way when you suggest they explore meditation, but if you can get them to give it a try, they will discover a practice to help them find peace and reduce stress. And it only has to be for a few minutes a day to be effective!

GUIDELINES

- **Explore some meditation practices for teens.** *There are plenty of meditation apps , like Insight Timer, online but a book like "Practicing Mindfulness" by Matthew Sockolov or "5 Minute Mindfulness Meditations for Teens" by Nicole Libin can be a great place to start.*
- **Begin practicing a few minutes a day.**

IV

Arts & Crafts Activities

Arts & Crafts Activities are all about learning new skills.

The projects in this section will help your teen to become comfortable learning to do something entirely new and to find ways to complete something even when it is a challenge.

56

Calligraphy

Calligraphy is a great art form for those of us who do not think of ourselves as artistic. It allows us to follow precise instructions while allowing our personalities to shine through into something beautiful.

All teens need to learn calligraphy is a pen and paper. After they have mastered the skill they can hire themselves out to address holiday cards and wedding invitations!

IDEAS

- **Use a complete calligraphy set to get started or just purchase a brush pen.** *Sets include pens and ink and a simple instruction booklet.*
- **To explore more of the art of calligraphy, there are many books on calligraphy and hand lettering.**
- **Calligraphy videos are also helpful in learning the art.**

57

Batik

Batik is decorative fabric technique from Indonesia. Patterns are created on the fabric with wax that resists the dye so that when it is washed away, the pattern remains un-dyed.

Teens can create their own batik fabric using flour paste instead of wax. Cloth napkins are a great first project but teens can batik clothes, sheets, and more!

INSTRUCTIONS FOR BATIK

- **Gather fabric to dye, fabric paint, flour, spray bottles (for each color paint) or sponge brush, and a squeeze bottle,**
- **Create a paste of one cup flour to one cup water.**
- **Use the squeeze bottle to "draw" on the fabric with the flour paste.**
- **Allow the paste to dry.**
- **Thin the paint so that it can be sprayed from the bottle.**
- **Spray the fabric with the paint. Use a single color or many.** *Or if using a brush, dab it on. Be sure to cover the work area and be careful not to break up the flour paste too much.*
- **Allow the paint to dry for a few hours.**
- **Use a bucket to soak the fabric to loosen and remove the flour paste.**
- **When most of the paste is gone you can wash the fabric.**

58

Quilting

Quilting can be not only a great solo project for a teen but also a fun family project (think quilting bee!).

Teens can make a very basic quilt with a few pieces of fabric and some basic sewing skills.

INSTRUCTIONS FOR MAKING A QUILT

- **Decide on the size of the quilt.** *A twin bed quilt is about 5 feet by 7 feet which is plenty big for a beginner!*
- **Pick the material for the quilt.** *A fun quilt for teens is to make it out of old, meaningful t-shirts.*
- **Cut the fabric into 6 inch squares. Decide how many squares are needed for the size of the quilt.** *It will be double if the back is also going to be patchwork.*
- **Decide on the pattern of the quilt.** *A random quilt is the easiest but if you want to make a particular pattern the best idea is to lay the squares out on the floor in the pattern you want.*
- **Begin sewing together each row.**
- **When all the rows are done, begin attaching them to each other in order.**

- **When finished, lay out the backing then lay on a layer of batting then lay on the top. Pin the three layers together all over the quilt.**
- **Trim the edges.**
- **Begin sewing along all of the seam lines between the squares until you have done every one!**
- **Trim the edges with bias tape.**

59

Screenprinting

Screenprinting lets us take a piece of art and put it on to a piece of fabric, like a t-shirt.

Teens can use an image they created or borrow from someone else and with a little ink, give it new life as a piece of wearable art. Screenprinted shirts are bags make really special, personal gifts.

IDEAS

- **A starter kit is a great idea.** *We loved the Speedball Introductory Screen-printing Kit. It comes with everything you need to get started except the fabric you will be printing on.*

60

Bookbinding

For Christmas one year, we made homemade journals for everyone. They loved them and learning how to put together a book the old-fashioned way was really special for us.

Teens can make books using only paper, a needle and thread. Homemade books make wonderful gifts or can be used for personal journals or sketchbooks.

IDEAS

- **Buy a bookbinding kit online or make one with a ruler, a knife, something sharp to poke holes, a needle and thread, a clamp and glue.**
- **Find a bookbinding tutorial online.** *I love "Bookbinding Tutorial" form thepostmansknock.com.*

61

Basket Weaving

Basket weaving is such a beautiful lost art. The process is simple enough for everyone to tackle and the idea of making something that will be used all the time is always appealing.

Teens can weave custom baskets as storage for their rooms.

IDEAS

- **Use a complete kit to get started.** *Reed and Cane's Introduction to Basket Weaving Kit is a great and inexpensive place to start.*
- **To explore more of the art of basket weaving, purchase the supplies and improvise on the basic techniques already learned.** *YouTube videos can help with some more advanced techniques.*
- **Another great method is to weave baskets with paper.** *There are plenty of tutorials on Pinterest to choose from.*

62

Whittling

Whittling is the process of taking a piece of wood and removing little bits of it to create a functional or decoration object. It does require a bit of practice to create things that look they way you want but the process is pretty addictive so most teens won't mind!

After just a little practice teens can whittle something as cool as a spoon!

IDEAS

- **Get a whittling knife.** *I also highly suggest a whittling glove to protect their hand!*
- **Learn some of the basic techniques.** *There is a YouTube Video "Whittling How to Get Started" or books like the "Complete Starter Guide to Whittling".*

63

Stained Glass

From cathedral windows to Tiffany lamps, stained glass can be found all around us.

While teens won't be able to create enormous windows or elaborate shade, they can easily learn to create simple items like suncatchers and vases.

IDEAS

- **Purchase a stained glass kit.** *They are a little expensive but include everything you need.*
- **Find simple beginner projects at first.** *The book "Stained Glass Projects for Beginners" by Lynette Wrigley offers lots of great and simple ideas.*
- **For an easier or less expensive project, do faux stained glass.** *They will need Simulate Liquid Leading and glass paint. They can then create any design they want by piping on the liquid leading and when dry, paint the sections.*

64

Tie Dye

Every few years, tie dying becomes a thing again. In my house, it has always been a fun summer activity and my teens tie dye everything from shirts to socks to comforters!

All teens need are some old clothes and a few packages of dye. While t-shirts are the old standard teens can feel free to add life to any solid colored item they want.

IDEAS

- **Purchase fabric dye.** *You can buy individual dyes or grab a tie dye kit with lots of colors.*
- **Tie up their items with rubber bands and apply the dye by dipping or using applicator bottles. Allow to dry and then rinse and wash.**
- **Look online for how to create different patterns.**

65

Bread Baking

There are few things more wonderful than the smell of freshly baked bread!

With just a little yeast, flour and water your teen can bring that delicious smell to your very own kitchen. And I promise that after you have had freshly baked bread, you will never need to go back to store bought!

IDEAS

- **Become familiar with the process and terms of bread making.** *Food Network has a great primer called "How to Bake Bread".*
- **Grab a bread cookbook or find recipes on online.** *I love James Beard's "Beard on Bread". It's a classic!*
- **The two best starter projects for teens are white or whole wheat sandwich bread or a French baguette.**
- **Sourdough is a whole new level of break baking so perhaps leave that to tackle a bit later!**

66

Knitting

I know knitting can sound kind of grandmotherly but if you can convince your teen to give it a try they will find it to be really relaxing!

Your teen just needs knitting needles, yarn, and a bit of quiet to get the hang of knitting. The next thing you know you all have new hats and scarves for winter!

IDEAS

- **Learn the basic knit and purl right online.** *Martha Stewart has a great primer on her site called "How to Knit".*
- **Start off with a simple project like a scarf.**
- **Stuck? Put out a call for help.** *There are plenty of people in the community who would love to share their knitting wisdom.*
- **If regular knitting is intimidating, try loom knitting.**

67

Embroidery

Embroidery is a great way for teens to learn the basic sewing skills they will need to sew on a button or mend a tear when they are grown and flown.

Teens need only a piece of fabric and some embroidery thread to get started.

IDEAS

- **The easiest way to start is to buy an embroidery kit.** *A kit includes a design printed on fabric, floss, a needle and instructions.*
- **Kits can be just samplers that you frame and hang on the wall or you can find more useful things like napkins and pillowcases.**

68

Jewelry Making

When your teen is itching to make something beautiful and unique, have them try their hand at making jewelry. It can be as simple as stringing beads onto a stretchy cord.

Teens can make jewelry from just some stretchy cord and beads. Or get even more creative using found items to make some real custom jewelry. *(My daughter once make earrings out of origami cranes!)*

IDEAS

- **Making simple bracelets with beads and stretchy cord is a great place to start.**
- **To get more advanced, visit the jewelry section of the craft store play around with all of the components to create necklaces, earrings and more.**

69

Ukulele Playing

While I tend to like quieter projects, playing an instrument is a wonderful skill to learn. And the ukulele is inexpensive and easy.

IDEAS

- Be sure your teen buys a ukulele music book with their ukulele.
- Once they have mastered the ukulele, your teen might want to move on to a more complex instrument like the guitar.

70

Origami

When my daughters read "Sadako and the Thousand Paper Cranes" they became immediate experts at folding origami cranes. Those cranes launched us in to trying our hand at different animals. First, that I could make little animals out of paper and second, that someone figured out how you make little animals out of paper!

Teens need only some household paper to get started. Once they get hooked they can string their animals into a sort of mobile if they want to keep them!

IDEAS

- **An origami kit is great but I really love the origami-a-day calendars.** *Each day you are treated to a new origami project. By the end of the year you have created some pretty fun origami.*
- **There are also lots of simple instructions online.**

71

Map Making

I feel a little sad for my teens that they will never have the joy of using a giant paper map to navigate their way somewhere new. Being the "navigator" is one of my fondest memories of my childhood and it may have inspired a slightly irrational love of maps in me!

Every time I see an old map, I think about what it took to create it and how amazingly accurate or inaccurate it might be. Having your teen try their hand at map making can be a really fun and unique project.

IDEAS

- Get inspired with the beautiful book "Maps: Their Untold Story" by Rose Mitchell.
- Use the book "Map Art Lap" by Jill Berry to prompt the creation of original maps.
- If map making isn't interesting to them, they can try using maps to make some art!

72

Weaving

I bought a loom a few years ago because I wanted to learn how to weave. My teens quickly became obsessed with the art and stole my loom!

Teens need only some leftover yarn and an inexpensive loom to get started. While scarves and place mats are simple projects to start with, teens can sew together woven pieces into things like tote bags or clothes.

IDEAS

- **Purchase a simple loom.**
- **Follow the instructions to weave a piece of fabric.**
- **Use yarn to weave.** *Or my favorite is to weave with strips of old fabric.*

V

Communications Activities

Communication Activities help teens learn to express themselves clearly and authentically, which to me, is one of the most important skills we can help our teens learn.

The projects in this section will help your teen to fine-tune their reading, writing, and listening skills.

73

Design a Website

Over the years I have built dozens of websites. Some for my own business adventures, some for local non-profits, some for friends, and some just for fun. It is a skill I am glad to have and one that I have encouraged my teens to build.

Teens can build a website for their art (like my one daughter has for her college art portfolio) or for a business or charity they run or even just for family photos or history. After they have fine-tuned their skills, they can offer to build websites for others, for fun or for profit.

GUIDELINES

- **Select a platform for the site**. *I am a big fan of Wix. It is easy to use, flexible, and you can have a free site.*
- **Decide what the site is going to be about.**
- **Look at lots of websites to see what they like and don't like.**
- **You can get crazy with web design but I encourage teens to just explore the layouts that are provided on the platform they choose and then learn to customize them by adding and removing parts.** *A web design class can also be valuable for teens who really want to learn how to do it.*
- **Learn how to build their website by exploring the educational materials**

provided by the platform. *Wix provides a great Wix Training Academy to get you started and keep you learning.*

74

Write an Urban Legend

An urban legend is a genre of folklore comprising stories circulated as true, especially as having happened to a friend or family member, often with horrifying or humorous elements. Writing their own is a great way to develop narrative and descriptive skills. And to scare their friends!

TIPS

- Be familiar with urban legends before trying to write one.
- Remember that urban legends are based on real life events, people, or circumstances. *People want to believe things that could be real.*
- Creating and describing a scary character, a setting, and a scary happening before sitting down to write is helpful.
- Try sharing the urban legend and see if it actually becomes legend!

75

Write a Movie Review

Everyone has an opinion about the movie they just saw. "That was awesome" or "That sucked." But actually writing a review guides teens to think about what caused them to form the opinion and encourages them to convey that others will understand.

TIPS

- Taking notes during the movie can be helpful.
- The review should give a little overview of the movie, what they liked and why, what they didn't like and why, and if they would recommend the movie.
- Reviews can be posted online at sites like IMDB.

76

Use Creative Writing Prompts

Creative writing not only helps tees to unleash their creative side, it helps them to feel more comfortable with writing in and about everyday life. Prompts can really help draw them into the process of writing each and every day.

TIPS

- **Don't be limited to just stories!** *Let the prompt inspire stories, poems, comics, essays, and more!*
- **There are tons of writing prompts online, come up with your own, or use the ones listed below.**
- **Sometimes setting a time limit can get the writing flowing.**

30 WRITING PROMPTS FOR TEENS
Be inspired by ...

1. The lyrics from your favorite song
2. Your favorite piece of clothing
3. Something that scares you
4. Aliens
5. A meme you saw today

6. The first human colony in space
7. Moving to a new town
8. Finding out you have a magical power
9. A world where we only communicate via social media
10. Sixty year old you
11. A monster
12. Two weather phenomena combining into an epic storm
13. A world without war
14. Your life if you turned into an animal
15. A family ghost
16. A famous artwork
17. Dinner with 5 interesting people
18. Living your entire life underground
19. A place you have always wanted to travel
20. A telephone call
21. Living your life but in a different historical period
22. An unlikely friendship
23. One event seen from multiple perspectives
24. A delivery person
25. Central Park
26. A viral social media post
27. A rumor
28. Camping
29. An everyday item
30. A secret

77

Write a Play

Writing a play is such a challenge! There is so much that needs to be conveyed only through dialogue and expression. It is a great lesson in observation and mindfulness!

TIPS

- A single scene or a short story is an easier project than a full length play.
- A storyboard can be helpful to understand the main point of each scene.
- A script describes the action and gives each character narration.
- Scripts are formatted in a certain way and teens can research online how this is done.

78

Write a Comparison

I find that most teens, well most people, are oblivious to why they prefer one thing to another. To help my teens learn to be more aware of their feelings, preferences and opinions, I let them eat cake. Well, tarts, actually. We tried tarts from different bakeries and ate them side by side, paying close attention to the similarities and differences and what motivated our choice of "best".

TIPS

- **Select products that are interesting to your teen. Like apps or cookie from a bakery.**
- **Be sure to pick items that are similar, like two tarts, not a brownie and a cookie.**
- **Creating a list beforehand of things that are important, is a good way to capture data.**
- **The written comparison can include an overview of the product type and the two products, it an describe the similarities and the differences, and it can include an assessment of which product is better.**

79

Create a Comic

Writing a comic is a great way to learn to distill a story down into only the most important ideas and the most impactful words.

TIPS

- **Comics can be drawn by hand or done online using free products like Storyboard That.**
- **Comics can tell an entire story or just share a quick thought.**
- **A storyboard can help organize longer comics.**

80

Write a Forensic Fairy Tale

One of my favorite homeschool assignments was having my kids rewrite classic fairy tales as "who done it's". It was a great exercise in really pulling out the important information from a story and then utilizing it in a new way.

TIPS

- Select a classic fairy tale.
- Re-write it keeping the bad guy a secret!
- Keep all the original characters.
- Keep the original flow of the story.
- Give at least 5 clues throughout the story.
- Include at least 2 misleading suspects.
- Reveal the criminal at the end of the story.

81

Go On a Newspaper Scavenger Hunt

Reading a real paper newspaper is a lost art! Get your teens excited to explore the paper by giving them a scavenger hunt. Prizes optional but highly encouraged!

TIPS

- **Have teens clip the items that they find and number them so you can easily tell what they found.**
- **Discussing what they found adds a little extra learning to this project!**
- **Create your own list or use the one below.**

SCAVENGER HUNT ITEMS

1. An article about someone who achieved something significant.
2. A story or ad that makes you laugh.
3. A typo or spelling error.
4. An article about a crime.
5. A recipe for a dessert
6. An article about a war.
7. A movie listing.

8. A story about someone over 60.
9. An ad for a local event.
10. An article about an election.
11. An article about a foreign country.
12. An article that makes you sad.
13. A comic.
14. An article about an athlete.
15. A photograph with a flag.
16. A weather report.
17. An article about an animal.
18. An article about the stock market.
19. A picture of someplace you have been.
20. An article about a local business.
21. A movie review.
22. An article about a restaurant.
23. An article with someone named Smith or Jones in it.
24. An ad for a car.
25. An article that makes you happy.

82

Write and Film a Commercial

When I recently wanted my teens to discuss their opinions on the deforestation of the rain forest, I asked them to communicate it in the form of a commercial. Not only did they need to form an opinion and gather supporting evidence, they needed to make it clear and engaging. In only 45 seconds!

TIPS

- **Commercials can be entertaining or emotional.**
- **Commercials should creative enough to make the viewer want to buy or hop on board.**
- **Explain to viewers what problem you are solving for them.** *They need to know why they should care!*

83

Start a Blog or Vlog

Blogging and vlogging are great ways for kids to show themselves to the world. They can entertain or educate or stand up for a cause that is meaningful to them.

TIPS

- **Picking a meaningful topic is important because it is hard to generate content around something that is not important to you.**
- **On most blog platforms you can block comments, if that is a concern.**
- **Set a reminder to create a post on certain days or after certain events.**

84

Write a Restaurant Review

Every time we take a bite of food we have an opinion. "Yum" or "Yuck". Writing a review of a meal helps teens to actually think about why they felt the way they did about their dining experience and encourages them to share it in a way that will be useful to others.

TIPS

- Taking notes during the meal can be helpful.
- The review should give a little overview of the restaurant, what they liked and why, what they didn't like and why, and if they would recommend the restaurant.
- Reviews can be posted online at sites like Yelp.

85

Create a Family Newsletter

A newsletter is a fun and creative way to keep far-away family updated on everything going on in your life. Especially the folks who don't get your daily Facebook posts!

TIPS

- **Most word processing applications offer a few newsletter templates to choose from.**
- **Not everything has to be a long article!** *Pictures, announcements, and even some silly ads make the newsletter more fun.*

86

Write to a Pen Pal

Throughout my teen years I had a pen pal from Malaysia, Winnie Lee. Winnie was a great sounding board for all my teen angst while also be a window into a world much bigger than my own. Once my own daughters were old enough, I arranged for them to have their own pen pals!

TIPS

· **Online sites like PenFriends and PenPalWorld can help match teens up with one or more pen pals.**

87

Research Your Family Tree

I have been working on my family tree for about 20 years but recently recruited my daughters to research along with me. I loved all the conversations it sparked and we even found lots of new information (as new records are being added all the time) like a photo of my great-great-grandfather in a Civil War uniform and the ship's manifest where my great-grandmother's onboard birth was handwritten in the margin! When you research and create a family tree, not only are you learning about your ancestors but you are capturing your history to share with future generations.

TIPS

- Use geneology software like Ancestry or MyHeritage or just create a tree on paper or in a spreadsheet.
- Records from the National Archives are free to access online and provide you with census records, immigration records, marriage records, and more.
- Don't underestimate the power of interviewing family members. They can give you a great outline of the last few generations and some great stories to boot!

88

Start a Journal

Keeping a journal is a practice that teens can carry into adulthood. It helps them to sort out their thoughts and get to know themselves better, two things that are a real benefit to a peaceful and joyful existence!

TIPS

- **They can certainly keep a journal on a computer but there is really something to writing thoughts out by hand.**
- **There are plenty of journals for sale that provide prompts or they can use a simple notebook and grab one of the prompts below.**

JOURNAL PROMPTS

1. What is the best compliment you have ever received?
2. What makes you nervous?
3. Talk about something you are proud of.
4. What is your favorite song and why?
5. If you could know one thing about the future, what would it be?
6. Describe a happy memory.
7. Where is your happy place?

8. What makes you mad?
9. What do you like the most about yourself?
10. What is something that went really well today?
11. If you could travel anywhere in the world, where would you go and why?
12. Talk about one item you can't live without.
13. List 10 things that make you smile.
14. What is your least favorite chore?
15. Who do you trust the most and why?
16. Describe yourself through someone else's eyes.
17. What is something you are working hard to improve upon?
18. If you could travel back in time to three years ago and visit your younger self, what advice would you give yourself?
19. What makes you sad?
20. List three things that you would do if you weren't afraid.
21. What are you afraid of failing at?
22. What's bothering you right now?
23. Who is your inspiration and why?
24. What is your greatest fear?
25. What do you think you life would look like if you didn't have anxiety or depression (or something else)?
26. What does your best day look like?
27. Write your eulogy for your funeral at age 100.
28. Name 15 songs that pick you up.
29. Write about three of your best talents.
30. Write about 10 things you are grateful for.

89

Write a "Letter to the Editor"

"Letters to the Editor" are one of the most widely read sections of a newspaper. Encouraging your teen to write one about something they feel passionate about gives them the opportunity to be heard in a real way.

TIPS

- "Letters to the Editor" describe the topic, explain why it is important, provide evidence, and state an opinion about what action should be taken.
- Editing is important!
- Letters can be sent to local papers but don't disregard national papers like the Washington Post and NY Times!

90

Apply for College Scholarships

If your teen is heading to college, scholarships are probably on your wish list. Many scholarships require teens to write short essays about why they deserve the scholarship. This project not only helps teens practice some communication skills but can make you a bit (or a lot) money too!

TIPS

- **Scholarships are not all academic.** *There is something for everyone so don't dismiss this project just because your teen does not have straight A's and AP credits!*
- **Pinterest is a great source of scholarship posts!**
- **An additional part of the project can be to have your teen research scholarships that might be a good fit.**

91

Write Your Hero's Journey

The hero's journey is the story of a hero who goes on an adventure, and in a decisive crisis wins a victory, and then comes home changed or transformed. Think Dorothy in "The Wizard of Oz" or Harry Potter or Katniss from "The Hunger Games". But fictional characters are not the only ones who go on hero's journeys. We all do.

TIPS

- **"The Hero's Guidebook: Creating Your Own Hero's Journey" by Zachary Hamby is a great place for teen's to learn about the hero's journey and learn how to write their own.**
- **The Reedsy blog also has an article called "Hero's Journey 101" that outlines the 12 steps of any hero's journey.**
- **For teens who aren't keen on writing themselves as the hero in their real life hero's journey, they can feel free to write a fictional hero's tale!**

92

Start a Book Club

I used to think that a book club sounded like hell on earth. That was before I joined one! I found that a book club is actually a great way to get yourself to read, to really think about what you read, and consider how it relates to your view of yourself and the world around you.

TIPS

- **Create a book club schedule that works for everyone and that meets on a regular day and not just when everyone is done with the book.** *Once a month or every six weeks is enough time for everyone to the read the book.*
- **Allow each member an opportunity to pick the book and lead the meeting.**
- **Open up discussion on the book or look online or in the back of the book for a list of discussion questions.**

93

Write Reviews for Experiences

Writing reviews is a great way to be a little more observant of the world around you. When you know that you are going to be reviewing your experience, you are more likely to pay attention to the finer details of your experience. And businesses LOVE positive reviews so not only is your teen improving their powers of observation and their writing skills, you are helping someone out!

TIPS

- **Reviews can be for museums, parks, tours, landmarks, classes, and more.** *Anyplace teens happen to go!*
- **TripAdvisor and Google Reviews are great places to submit reviews. Or check the website of the business and see if they take direct submissions.**
- **A review can include the details of the experience and what your teen really enjoyed.** *It can also include things a person might want to know before they go.*
- **If your teen has something negative to say, encourage them to be kind and focus on improvement not criticism.**

94

Read to a Library Program

Communication skills don't just mean writing skills. Being able to speak in front of an audience is just as important. Starting out by reading at a library program is a great way to get used to being in front of an audience.

TIPS

- Most libraries have reading programs for kids but teens can also contact their local school or even read at a nursing home.
- Preview the book before reading it to a group.
- Introduce the book to the group and explain why it was chosen.
- Read with expression.
- Be prepared to answer questions!

95

Write a Guest Blog Post

So many times my homeschooled teens have't given their best effort because they know I am the only one who will read what they write. Letting them know that their writing is going to appear on a well-read blog really motivates them to up their writing game.

TIPS

- **Teens can certainly contact a blog they follow to see about writing a guest post but Elephant Journal is a great place to submit posts if you don't have that connection.**
- **Blog posts can be about anything!** *Just be interesting and authentic.*

96

Write a Horror Story

Horror is great genre to really get the creative juices flowing. It requires detailed descriptions to really set the mood and over the top scenarios are allowed because there can certainly be some fantasy element.

TIPS

- **Figuring out the fear is key! Is it something normal like bugs or heights or something supernatural like a zombie or vampire.**
- **Figure out what's at stake.** *The character's very survival? The safety of loved ones? Solving a mystery?*
- **Writing from the first person perspective really puts the reader in the place of fear.**
- **The more description, the scarier the story.** *So describe every creak, breath, and step!*

97

Start a Sketchbook

A sketchbook sounds like it is only something an artist would use but it is a great tool for anyone to capture their observations about themselves and the world around them in a visual way.

TIPS

- **Sketchbooks can be filled with drawings and paintings but can also include college, photographs, word art, poetry and more.** *It is really just a creative journal.*
- **Fill the sketchbook by using prompts or just by daily inspiration.**

SKETCHBOOK PROMPTS

Create art inspired by ...

1. A favorite place
2. A favorite color
3. Something big and something small
4. Black
5. A random word in the dictionary
6. A body part

7. Anger
8. Something hidden
9. History
10. Feathers
11. A page in a magazine
12. Food
13. An animal
14. Chains
15. A smell
16. Light
17. An ink blot
18. Matisse
19. A book you love
20. Shades
21. Keith Haring
22. The dark
23. Death
24. Water
25. Something that glows
26. A storm
27. Strings
28. A tattoo
29. A thumbprint
30. Watercolors
31. White

98

Write a Myth

Myths are as old as mankind. Some myths serve to explain how the world works and others provide an example of how to live a "good" life. All are written in a way that engages the reader in the lesson while keeping them interested enough to keep the story with them forever. Writing a new myth allows teens to take a look at something they want to explain and make sense of it in a creative and exciting way.

TIPS

- **Myths can be set in modern times!** *Lessons about how to stand up to bullies or why TikTok is all the rage are just two ideas!*
- **To make it a myth teens will need a "god" to help "man" learn the lesson they are teaching.** *They can use existing gods or create their own.*

99

Write a Manual

One of my very favorite assignments in college was to write a manual. It was meant to be a short project but I loved it so much that I created an entire book devoted to cycling trips in New Jersey and gave it to all my cycling friends! A manual is a great communication assignment because it requires us to really think through how something gets done in order and then explain it very clearly to another person.

TIPS

- **A big guide or a small instruction sheet are both perfectly good projects!**
- **It is imperative for teens write a manual about something they know how to do!!!** *If they can't do it, they can't explain it!*
- **Before writing the manual you can help your teen to understand how important clear and correct instructions are by asking your teen to write the instructions for making a peanut butter and jelly sandwich.** *And then making it by following their instructions to the letter! You most likely won't have a knife or have unscrewed the jar lids or have the right sides of the sandwich together! It's a fun and informative exercise.*

Made in the USA
Middletown, DE
23 November 2020